that and that and this and that
and far — over [barcode] r there
no and maybe ar [D1314129] perhaps
and tomorrow again hen and
and now and now — right now.
maybe not always and then and again
and nowhere everything, everything,
ing, sometimes OK and then not
and then and now and yes yes yes
again, always again and never
and never again again and again
, today and then and now right now,
always again again again again now
ything fast, everything, everything,
s, big things round, flat square,
where at once — now and again — now
everything everything all things
e always at once all things going
up and round round round into all
very bit of everything all now
now and forever always now.
d that into all that and this into, in,
n and then all from now — now
g now and more and now and more
thing and more now right now now
always and everything and always now

JIM HODGES

IAN BERRY and RON PLATT

with an essay by ALLAN SCHWARTZMAN

THE FRANCES YOUNG TANG TEACHING MUSEUM AND ART GALLERY

AT SKIDMORE COLLEGE

WEATHERSPOON ART MUSEUM

THE UNIVERSITY OF NORTH CAROLINA AT GREENSBORO

YOU ORNAMENT THE EARTH

A Dialogue with JIM HODGES by Ian Berry

Jim Hodges transforms ordinary objects into poignant art. Likened to souvenirs of lived experience, his work exposes the innate potential in familiar things such as silver chain, silk scarves, cut mirrors, colored lightbulbs, and aluminum foil. These delicate and sometimes ephemeral artworks mark the passage of time, compelling us to reflect on our own experiences of love, loss, memory, and longing. Despite the diverse media, styles, and techniques Hodges employs, a poetic sensibility and craft aesthetic consistently characterize his practice. As he cuts, reassembles, pins, stitches, and draws with his materials to create formally minimal visual meditations, subtle details of life come into focus.

IAN BERRY This exhibition brings together your early work with several examples of current projects. When you began making work what was driving you?

JIM HODGES It's hard to remember really. As a young artist I'm sure I was more concerned about what people were thinking about me than what I was thinking about! I was starting out, trying to shake off all the stuff I had picked up in art school and trying to find my voice. I was definitely thinking a lot about what was going on around me. I was experimenting with materials, and I felt it was important to find my place in the lineage of art history. I was settling into ideas about time and experience.

IB I think you are still experimenting with those ideas. Each exhibition you present seems to be another form of collaboration—if not an overt collaboration, then we are welcomed into your work and invited to participate as viewers. How much do you think about what someone is going to do in front of your work while you are making it?

(title page)
Untitled (Threshold), 1993–1994
silk, plastic, thread
and steel wire
92 x 58"
The Ann and Mel Schaffer
Family Collection

(facing page)
A Possible Cloud, 1993
cotton, silk flowers
24 x 24'
Collection of Todd Sturm

One, 1987
charcoal on paper
with staples
30 x 36 x 36"

JH I don't think that I am ever not engaged with that consideration. This dialogue or this interaction with a viewer, what's being perceived, what's being experienced, what's being responded to...

IB So you agree that viewers bring your works to life?

JH Actually, the viewer completes the work.

IB Drawing continues to be a consistent activity for you even as you push it into several different final products. Why did you choose the drawing *One* as your first mature work and how do you think it connects to what you have made since?

JH I had made many other things before I made *One*, but I guess it was the range of activity or the range of potential within that work that made it pivotal. It functioned on a number of levels, starting as a drawing—charcoal on paper. Then, the paper having physical qualities or characteristics that can be exploited, such as stapling it together to create a cylinder. Finally, it was dictating a particular motion or movement for the viewer. You have to be in constant movement to be able to see the work, so it would have a sense of life as a living material.

IB Viewers needed to complete the work.

JH Exactly. I had arrived at a place where I was interacting with viewers, or with the presumed viewer, and also with materials in a personal way. I made *One* and it was accidentally destroyed. I made it again without any charcoal on the paper—just the paper itself, like a ghost of the first one.

IB And it would still function in the space.

JH Right. It also answered other needs, a lot of requirements that I was asking of myself at the time, which is, where it is my work existed within space and how the drawing could be moved off the wall and put on the floor. I began using other planes in the environment and not just the wall. These are assignments that I had been giving myself on my way towards developing my own language or my own way of working.

I am always engaged with interaction, and with *One* it was walking around in a circle. Years later I made work that was about turning one's head 360 degrees, in turn drawing a line 360 degrees. In my work it all comes back to where my eyes take me. I know my systems, or my practice, in retrospect more than I do in terms of what's going to happen. In retrospect I can look back and say "here's this pattern that's exposed here, or here's this system working."

Untitled, 1988
mixed media
Dimensions variable
Studio view, New York
Destroyed

IB That suggests you are truly collaborating with your viewers because you give up part of the understanding of the work, and certainly every artist does that to a certain extent, but you are embedding it in a more integral way. You are being a very honest and welcoming collaborator and you let that influence the way you think as opposed to just one particular installation or one particular site.

JH You know it's very interesting, Ian, because each installation offers it own difficulties and also its own potential for how one makes something. I try to keep myself open for those potentials where I can see a crack, where I can slip in and maybe expand something for myself

IB That seems to be the key as opposed to any one color or subject or media, that truly connects all of your work—it's a continual conversation, a dialogue. Let's go back in time again. Another impor-tant moment for your career as an artist was when you worked for the New York collector, Elaine Dannheisser. During that time you were able to not only interact with a lot of different kinds of artwork, but interact with many of the best artists working at the time. Do any of these experiences remain as important models for you now?

JH A work by Christian Boltanski had a big impact on me. His piece was made of a group of metal boxes that stack on top of each other. Electric lights hung off the wall and illuminated black and white photographs of people above each stack. To install the work I had to open the metal boxes and put nails through the holes that were existing in the box. Inside each box was a copy of the portraits that were hanging on the outside. I was shocked to find the photos inside, and I was also very moved. It was profound for me. I appreciated the private, spiritual component in the work. I interpreted this as an intimate gesture by the artist, and I think that opened something up for me.

Latin Rose, 1990
tape and tar paper
72" diameter
Collection of the artist

IB You were a young artist in New York at the time, how did you meet her Mrs. Dannheisser?

JH I had a job when I was in graduate school as an art preparator working three days a week at the Nancy Hoffman Gallery in SoHo. One night there was an opening at the New Museum for performance artists, one of whom was Linda Montano. She was in the window of the museum, which was painted magenta that night, and she was reading palms for people. It was a big New York opening, packed with people milling around, and I was standing in line waiting to get my palm read. I look up and the crowd is parting for this woman who has a green velvet turban on, the image that I have of her is probably much more outrageous than she probably really looked, but it was quite beautiful and dramatic. She walked right up to me and asked, "How long is this going to take?" I had been standing there for quite a while and I estimated that it was about five minutes per person. I said, "Well, I'd say about five minutes per hand and there are five people ahead of you, so about a half-hour." She said "Oh, I don't want to stand around here, I want to go look at the art." So I said "Well, you go look at the art, I will hold your place for you, and when you come back you can do the same for me." She said, "Oh, you are very nice," and then turned around and walked away. When she returned I was at the front of the line and told her she could go first. For a few minutes we ended up talking and she asked me if I was an artist. It was 1986.

IB The same year you graduated from Pratt.

JH Yes, it was late winter or early spring of that year. I had graduated in the winter. Elaine asked if I had a studio. I told her that I had just gotten out of graduate school and that I was working in my bedroom in Brooklyn. She explained that she had a collection and a foundation in Tribeca and that she gave artists studio spaces in exchange for helping her with the collection. She asked if that would be something that I would be interested in. Of course I said, "yes!" We exchanged numbers and addresses that night. Later, I had a great palm reading by Linda Montano.

IB She said your future was bright?

JH She was amazing. She sat across the table and took both of my hands in her hands and looked at them and then looked me right in the eye and said, "don't be afraid to be traditional, don't worry about not being hip, don't worry about not being outside, just be yourself." A few weeks later Elaine called and she and Werner, her husband, drove me down to Tribeca and showed me the foundation. They took me downstairs and showed me this huge studio space and asked me if thought I could work there. I said "yes," and she gave me the keys. I was there for nine years. It was a real New York experience and one of the most important times of my life. My experience at the foundation is where my real education took place. I kind of dismantled myself, disassembled everything and put myself back together in working order.

IB What kind of education do you mean?

JH The Dannheisser Foundation was a very exciting place to be in. Sometimes it would get very over the top. Elaine liked things on the edge and appreciated pushing buttons. She would laugh at some of the responses people would have to the works she installed. So as I was working with Elaine upstairs, putting together these intense installations, my own work was developing in the basement. My underground studio was a crazy laboratory. "Making mulch," is how I would sometimes describe the process.

IB You started making art that is intimate without being overly didactic or autobiographical. You continue to make abstract work in which many want to find your biography. How overt do you intend to be in your works about personal experiences?

JH It's all personal. When I was younger I read Genet, learning about the struggles he went through to get his books written, then to get them out of prison and then to keep them on the book-shelves. There are many layers, walls that we continually have to tear down, personally and socially. In "Our Lady of the Flowers," Genet made an observation about the simple pleasure of seeing a stream of blue ribbon billowing in the air and the lace under a dress saying, there was no greater pleasure than these simple deli-cate details. Obviously, not a direct quote, but when I read those few lines, I felt such identification with his nature. I found myself in his words and what he was identifying as beauty and pleasure. I guess it was then that I started putting myself out there in my work. As simple and direct as I can.

IB I think you are being plain in a way that some Minimalists talked about materials—remove what doesn't need to be there, reduce the thing to what is the most important. You are also honoring the tradition of conceptual art. Seminal works by Sol Lewitt and Robert Morris often started with record keeping. It is an elemental process stripped of all excess where one can communicate clearly. Your piece, *A Diary of Flowers*, is a marriage of sorts of late twentieth century art history and your understanding yourself in a beautiful way, where your rigorous art thinking is seamless with your heartful life.

What's left, 1992
clothing with white brass chain
Dimensions variable
Collection of the artist

JH These moments matter and the record is important. Making *A Diary of Flowers* helped me understand myself. What is important to hold on to? Choosing a narrow range, such as flowers drawn on paper napkins, allowed me to explore my nature.

IB It is amazing to look at those pieces and see how many different views there are. Particularly in some of the bigger groupings there seems to be a thousand hands drawing those flowers. It is a perfect conceit to describe the way that these moments are unique, that there is something different about each one.

JH The range of the drawings is a record of many distinct events. I was really trying to be true to the moment and draw what came in the moment. Often I would look down at the napkin and the drawing would simply reveal itself. I would just "trace" what was already there. I think this happens often for artists, our work waits for us.

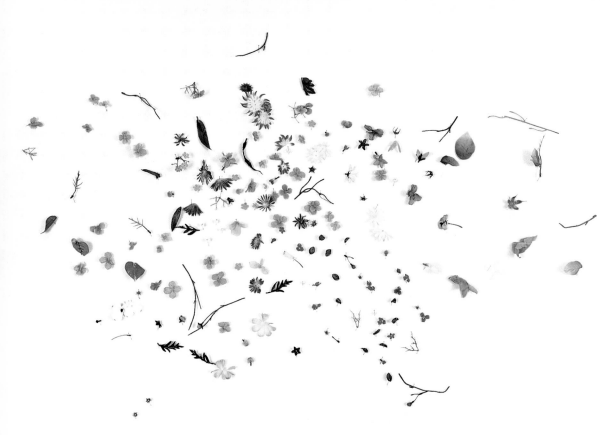

IB So you made *A Diary of Flowers* for three years in different places and different permutations, and it became a project of sorts, of learning how to be site-specific.

JH I had been thinking about "sites" for my work, but the diary really wasn't a project of learning to be site-specific. When I met Richard, Carla, and Glenn they had a lovely little gallery on East 71st Street. When they offered me my first one-person show, I had been working on the diary of flowers for some time and it was my intention to show one major work as my first exhibition. Their gallery was exactly the type of space I was looking for. It was a parlor floor of a town house. It even had a fireplace. I felt that the diary should be experienced so that you would be surrounded by it. The combination of size and "personality" of CRG's space was perfect.

IB It was the right scale...

JH It was perfect—domestic and elegant, yet modest in scale. That show was important in terms of how people starting knowing my work, although the first time I showed those drawings was in a group show at White Columns.

IB After that you started making flower pieces that were physical objects.

JH Right. My friend, Felix Gonzalez-Torres, had a show at the Fabric Workshop in Philadelphia and invited me to go down with him for the opening where I met the director, Kippy Stroud. A few months later I was invited to do a project with the workshop.

IB And the Fabric Workshop is where you worked out the first flower curtain?

JH Yes, the first curtain was made with the workshop. I had been playing around with silk flowers in my studio—taking them apart, pinning them on walls, making drawings with them. When the opportunity came to make something with the Fabric Workshop I was ready. I had this idea of returning the flowers back to fabric. I was interested in the history of each petal. How the material had been transformed; cut, painted, sculpted, and given a flower identity. I wanted to re-establish the material's fabric nature. I had sewn a small sample of what I wanted to make—a ratty looking scrap that Kippy laughed at. Merrill Mason was the project coordinator from the workshop and she established a method to fabricate a very large piece. The scale of these pieces was very important to me. I wanted them to be too big for the room. The way the curtains are introduced into space is important too. They are meant to hang in a space so that two spaces are created—soft architecture that creates a here and there. They should hang from the ceiling and touch the floor, and there should be excess pooled on the floor. I love the idea that they don't fit.

IB You have made ten curtains and many hands touch those pieces while you make them. Some of them became monochromes, white or black, and these colors change the spaces that they are in dramatically.

JH When I stopped painting I stopped working with color. Color was reintroduced in my work when I started using the fabric flowers. The first curtain, *every touch*, was assembled with a random placement. I made the first monochrome one, *Already Here, Already There*, for a show at CRG in 1995. It was all white. I showed it with the canvas piece, *stay close*. I also made a tiny white book with Julie Ault for that show and I inserted color pages to accompany her text. When Felix saw the white curtain he asked, "Can you do it in blue?" *In Blue* was the next one I made. With the little book and the curtains I started using color symbolically. I finished the flower curtains with a black one called *The end from where you are*.

Slowing Time, 2001
mirror on canvas
48 x 109"
Private Collection, Belgium

IB Your white curtain dissolves into pure light, and the black one becomes a heavier, dark presence, and lately your work has investigated light and color, spectra and reflective light, and the colors that are found in reflections. In some ways the curtains almost direct us to the spots of light that come through.

JH When I would look at the curtains installed I saw the energy coming from the part that wasn't there, the light coming through the holes.

IB Is light an important subject in your recent work?

JH Light has always been an inspiration, perhaps of late it is more apparent. I think it's most about subtle details and life experiences.

IB Camouflage has resurfaced in some of your wall paintings and mirror pieces. Mirrors themselves function as camouflage as much as the flower curtains function as camouflage, creating a kind of camouflage for the spaces that they are in. They all work to hide and reveal. Do you also see the mirrors and the flower curtains functioning as gallery camouflage?

JH Not necessarily, though that is an interesting read. Camouflage is a rendering of nature. This is what really attracted me to it and still does. It is a manmade depiction of nature by the artist Abbott Thayer. He made this observation about animal concealment and goes on to render nature in this simple reduced pattern of shadows—light and dark. I enjoy working with its source, which is nature, and then the issues that have been layered on it politically and culturally. I like loaded materials.

In all these works I try to be simple and direct. I try to get to a point where I am turning a material in a way so that something else is seen, an unfolding of the material to see what's there. It's about discovery.

IB You quoted a song lyric to me once in your studio that included the line "you ornament the earth...."

JH "Emmie" by Laura Nyro. It's a beautiful song, a love song. It's a song of appreciation, gratitude, and praise. I am moved by the poetry and inspired by the artist's perception and her clarity. Mostly I'm inspired by her generosity, her honesty, and her expression of love. I don't remember why I mentioned it, but I know as a goal "ornamenting the earth" seems like a great target—you know, celebrating being here.

Untitled, 2001
Prismacolor on wall
Dimensions variable
Installation views,
CRG Gallery, New York

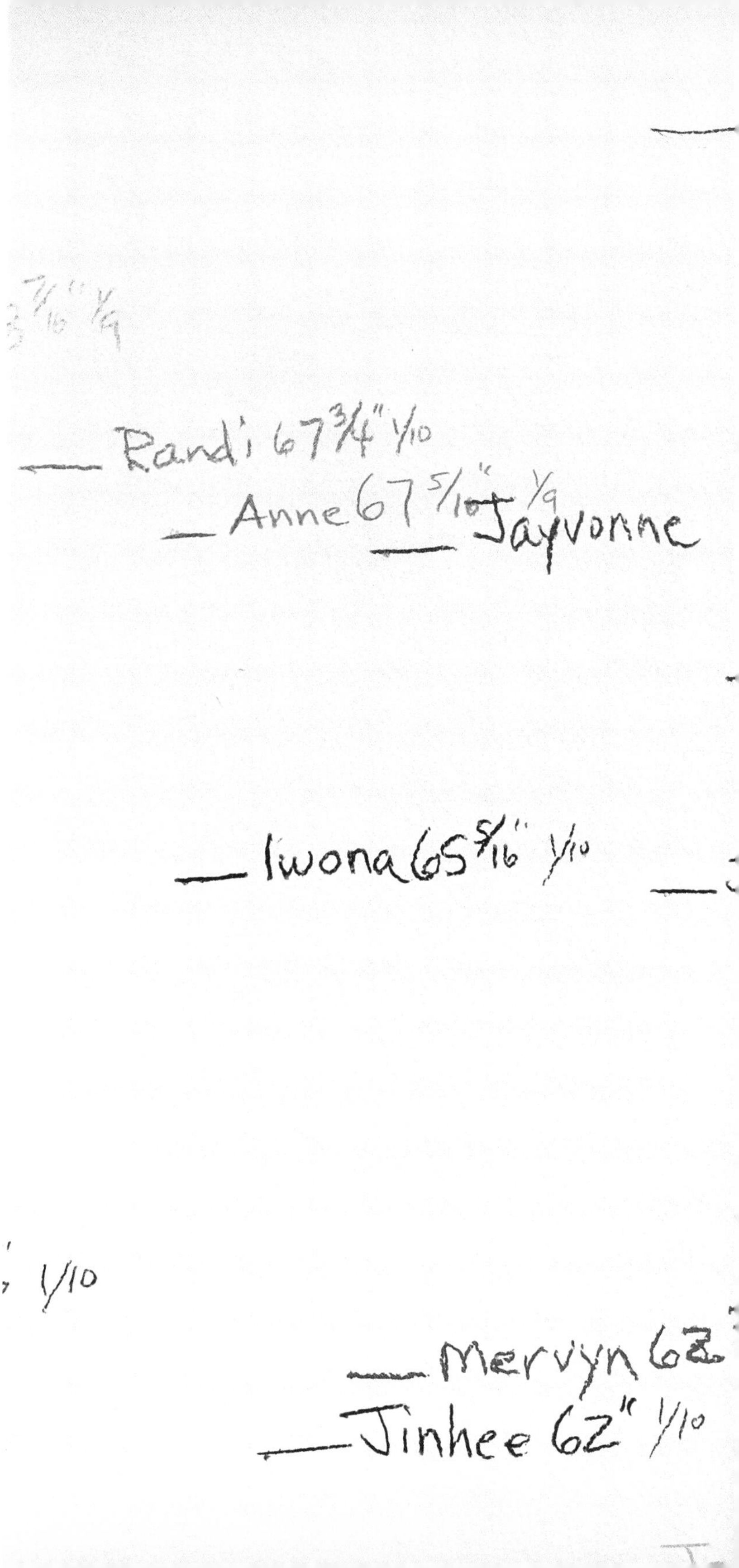

$3\frac{3}{16}" \frac{1}{9}$

___ Randi $67\frac{3}{4}" \frac{1}{10}$

___ Anne $67\frac{5}{16}" \frac{1}{9}$ Jayvonne

___ Iwona $65\frac{9}{16}" \frac{1}{10}$ ___

Wherever you like, (Possible Drawing), 1999 (detail)
Prismacolor on wall
Dimensions variable
Installation view, *Jim Hodges*, Miami Art Museum, 1999

, $\frac{1}{10}$

___ Mervyn 62
___ Jinhee $62" \frac{1}{10}$

—Phil 70

68¾" 1/12

Buzz → 69½ 1/17

—John

—Maranda 6

1/14

—Jerry 67⁵⁄₁₆" 1/

—Jessica 66¾" 1/13   —Ca

incent 66½" 1/12
Rudy 66⁵⁄₁₆" 1/9
Gael 65¹⁵⁄₁₆" 1/10
Hisao 65¹¹⁄₁₆" 1/12
65¼" 1/9

—Trudi 65⅛"

—Sue 64⁵⁄₁₆" 1/14 I
—Kristen 63⅞" 1/11
—Deana 63⅞

—Susan 62¹⁄₁₆" 1/10

6.1⅛" 1/9

Gate, 1991
steel, aluminum, copper,
and brass chain with blue room
78 x 60"
Installation view,
White Columns, New York
Collection of the artist

A Diary of Flowers, 1994 (detail)
ink on paper napkins
with pins in 565 parts
Dimensions variable
Carlos and Rosa de la Cruz
Collection

stay close, 1995
pre-stretched, pre-primed canvases,
steel bolts
120 x 120 x 60"
Courtesy of the artist and
CRG Gallery, New York

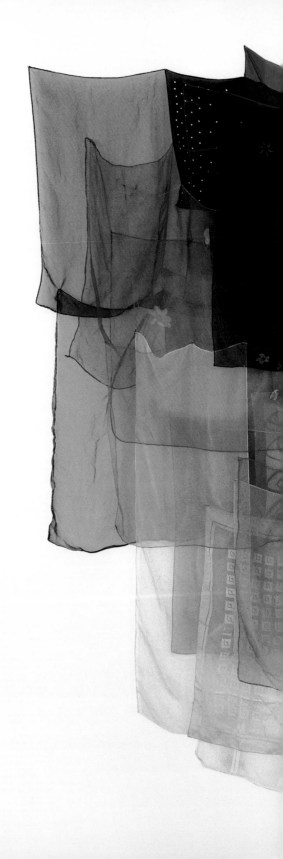

With the wind, 1997
scarves, thread
90 x 99 x 5"
Collection of Penny Cooper
and Rena Rosenwasser

26

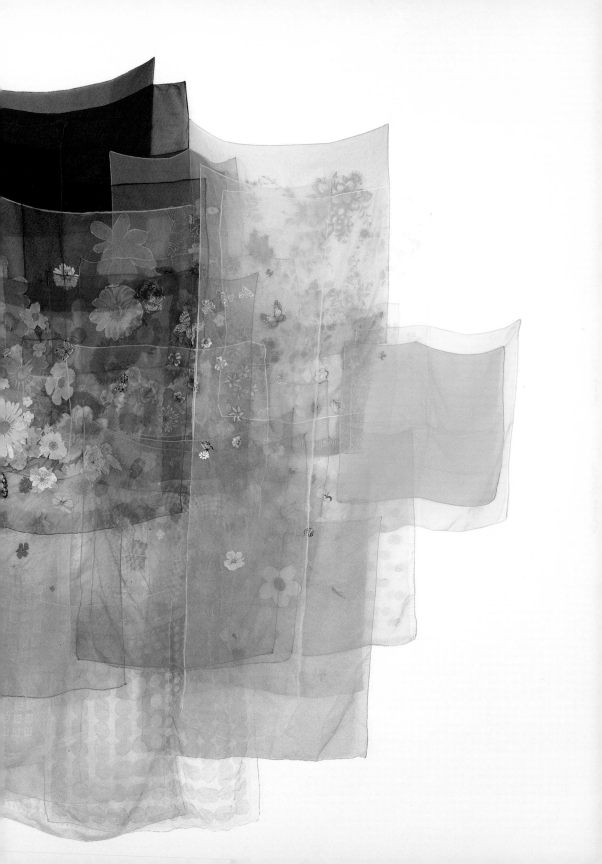

on we go, 1996
metal chain with pins
57 x 48 x 22"
Collection of Eileen and
Peter Norton, Santa Monica

Blurring, 1997
white brass chain
36 x 36 x 6"
Collection of Ann and
Ron Pizutti

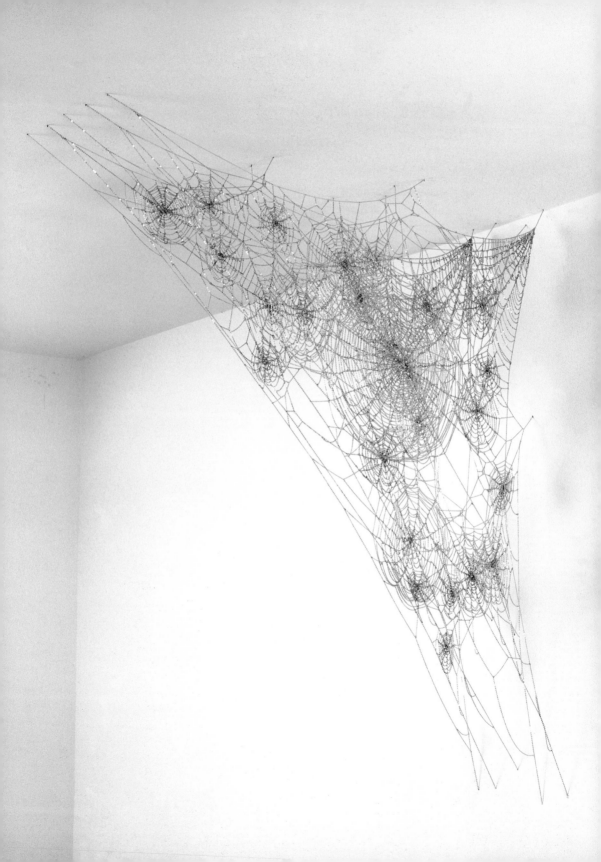

Folding (into a greater world), 1998
mirror on canvas
72 x 96"
Collection of Eileen and
Peter Norton, Santa Monica

Where are we now?, 1999
silk, cotton, polyester, and thread
24 x 18'
Installation view, *Jim Hodges*,
Miami Art Museum, 1999
Carlos and Rosa de la Cruz Collection

(overleaf, detail)

34

When the light comes on, 1998
cotton and polyester
48 x 32 x 1.75"
Bob Rennie/Rennie Management
Corporation Collection, Vancouver

Landscape, 1998
cotton, silk, wool, plastic, and nylon
64 x 34 x 6.5"
Collection of Eileen and
Peter Norton, Santa Monica

(facing page, detail)

As close as I can get, 1998
Pantone color chips with
adhesive tape
81 x 81"
Collection of Eileen and
Peter Norton, Santa Monica

(overleaf)
Coming through, 1999
lightbulbs, ceramic sockets,
wood and metal panels
31 x 63 x 5"
Collection of Rebecca and
Alexander Stewart, Seattle

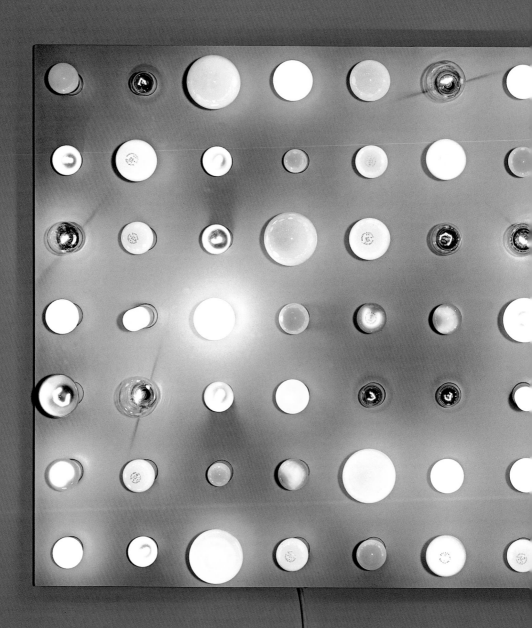

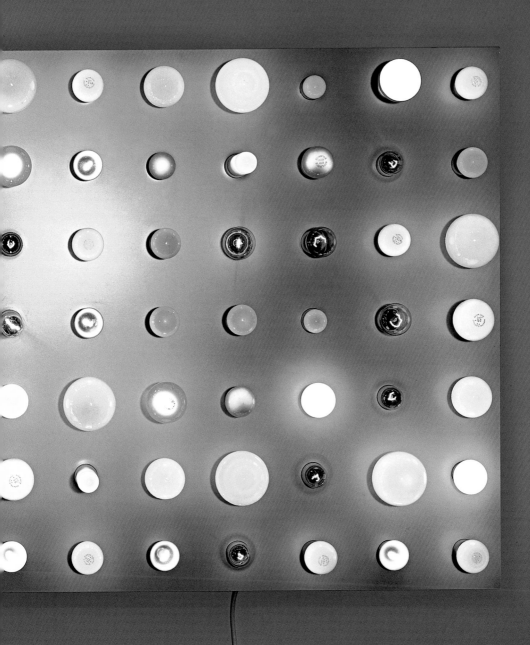

Happy/Sunrise-Sunset
("In the Beginning is My End"
—T.S. Eliot), 2001
Prismacolor on paper
47.5 x 35"
Private Collection

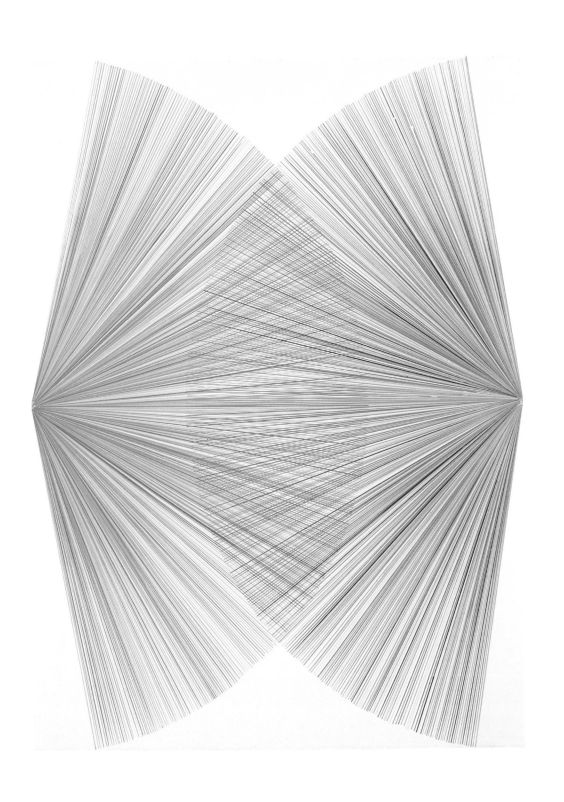

I SEE THE LIGHT by Ron Platt

Jim Hodges' primary impulse as an artist is to communicate. His exquisitely crafted works beckon our senses first, then our intellect. Hodges distills his emotional and intellectual experiences into a broad range of art forms and materials. Yet, for all its eclecticism, his artistic practice maintains an underlying personal and formal coherence. In fact, the diversity of Hodges' art sets up a kind of free-flowing dialogue among the works, one that draws in those who encounter them more as participants than viewers.

Like that of many artists today, Hodges' work does not fit into neat categories of style or subject matter. Trained as a painter, he has maintained the visceral pleasures of that process in work that draws from such sources as feminism and gender politics, litera- ture, and the natural world. Stylistically, it encompasses decorative excess and the restraint and refinement of minimal and post- minimal art. Aiming to communicate in direct and essential ways, Hodges uses a vocabulary of straightforward techniques to bring out the inherent beauty and possibility of manufactured, everyday materials. He has said, "I search for methods and materials that can be implemented with the slightest gesture to yield the most meaning. Everything is available in the work itself, there is nothing hidden," and yet, explicitly personal content and meaning are not easily perceived in the work. Instead, its poetic ambiguity elicits a viewer's own experiences and understanding.

This essay focuses on a selection of Hodges' work from the last ten years, in which light is a primary component. Hodges approaches light in myriad ways and to greatly divergent meanings and effects. He uses it physically, as material; conceptually, as symbol or metaphor; and for narrative, as subject. Throughout his photographs, lightbulb sculptures, mixed media and Prismacolor works on paper, Prismacolor wall-drawings, mirror "paintings," and

Ultimate Joy, 2001
lightbulbs, ceramic and plastic sockets, wood and metal panels
32 x 64 x 9"
Collection of Linda Pace

three-dimensional chain "drawings," light is a common denominator. When considering these works together, one becomes gradually aware of how skillfully Hodges taps into light's wide-ranging associations to time, energy, movement, and notions of ephemerality.

As a material, light is mutable and responsive. Natural or artificial, it fades, casts shadows, activates and blends colors, reflects, reveals, or blinds. It can entice or repel. Light represents spirit, energy, inspiration, and hope. It enables us to reference and track time, from its travel through the universe, to the sun's marking of the day. One is cognizant of its movement, and how it shadows our own.

Whether intended or not, light is an ingredient of all but the most conceptual art. Historically, the representation of light in Western art was meant to portray spirituality or divinity. Early American landscape painters used light to convey nature's majesty, while the Impressionists, attuned to late nineteenth-century developments in mathematics and what would come to be called physics, were intrigued with its intellectual and perceptual properties. The years since then have been marked by rapid and unprecedented developments in science and technology. (Consider that only eighty years separate Edison's invention of the lightbulb in 1879 and the introduction of the laser.) Artists have kept pace, and as they transformed notions of aesthetic style, content, and form, they have investigated and exploited light's essential nature both through traditional artforms and through film, photography, fluorescent and neon tubing, and even the sun's rays.

Light has been essential to the work of such contemporary artists as James Turrell, whose installations manipulate natural and artificial light to heighten viewers' perceptions and to prompt their reflection. Dan Flavin enhanced Minimalism's emphasis on the here and now with his elegant configurations of fluorescent lightbulbs. Jeff Wall's monumental photographs in lightboxes exploit the allure of contemporary

A play of light, 2001
alumnium foil on paper
30 x 33.5″
Collection of Rebecca and
Alexander Stewart

advertising and cinema. Nancy Holt created site-based sun tunnels that enlisted the actual sunlight to focus attention on time and location. Photographer Hiroshi Sugimoto's subtle seascapes and images of glowing movie house screens create magic with available light. Each of these artists emphasize particular aspects and qualities of light in their art, while Hodges' approach to light is holistic, incorporating these and many more of its characteristics into his practice.

Hodges seems particularly attuned to the sensory world—a perspective developed through his early and prolonged affinity to the natural world. Raised in Spokane, Washington, Hodges describes his boyhood self as, "a kid who grew up in the woods and spent many hours drawing from nature, looking up into the trees. I remember marveling at how the sunlight bent shadows around the craggy trunks of the pine trees." Such intimate early rapport with nature's forms and forces would have a causal effect on his artistic practice.

From the beginning, Hodges' art has evolved out of intuitive play and investigation. In his basement studio at the Dannheisser Foundation in the late 1980s, he studied the reflections and shadows produced by candles and mirrors, and made drawings and installations in response. These early experiments already exhibited the artists' attention to some of the pivotal themes of his mature work: time, ephemerality, and illusion. During this period, he was also exploring the fundamental properties and characteristics of commercially made materials such as Scotch tape, tarpaper, and metal jeweler's chain.

From the chain he began to fashion "spiderwebs," thus extending his drawing practice into three-dimensions and providing a subject rich with associative meanings. The 1996 sculpture, *on we go*, is an assembly of seven progressively-sized webs; each crafted from metal chain. The piece is suspended in a corner by pins, with the smallest web closest to the corner and the largest farthest out. The piece offers multiple effects from different perspectives. From one vantage point the individual webs seem to converge into a glinting core of light; from another angle, they are seen in their

Ahhhh, 2000
lightbulbs, ceramic sockets,
wood and metal panels
45 x 35 x 20"
Marieluise Hessel Collection on
permanent loan to the Center for
Curatorial Studies, Bard College,
Annadale-on-Hudson, New York

54

sequential order; from yet another they look like an intricate schematic drawing—perhaps representing Hodges' process of developing and connecting strands of thought into a complex circuitry of ideas.

Throughout the 1990s, Hodges regularly addressed notions of time and impermanence. In 1993, he made a work that embodied the fleeting nature of existence for his close friend and fellow artist, the late Felix Gonzales-Torres. *A slow sunset* comprises twenty-four candles of varying sizes. The tallest candle is black, while the rest are the colors of a sunset. According to Hodges, he and Gonzalez-Torres shared a similar romantic tendency, "We were drawn to one another personally because of our similar natures. He had a great influence on me." The two certainly concurred upon the importance of the audience to their work. Gonzalez-Torres made literal the notion of participation and exchange in his stacks of posters or piles of individually wrapped candies by inviting viewers to take pieces of his work away with them. In a similar vein, Hodges claims that the subject of his art is most often the viewer him— or herself, an idea he makes manifest in works created with commercial mirror.

In mirror, Hodges discovered a material loaded with qualities and associations that suited his approach. His first mirror works, created in 1996, were whole panels that he secured to backings and broke from behind with a hammer. This action created a network of fissures across the mirror's surface. To Hodges, these works represented a break from his past.

Hodges' mirror works have two essential components: the viewer, and light itself. He is drawn to what he calls the mirror's "live quality...how a mirror is affected by the changing light of day." Yet the works are incomplete until the viewer steps before them. Each viewer brings his or her own unique presence to the work, and as such, participates in the structure of its meaning.

The mirror mural, *Folding (into a greater world)*, 1998, is created from tiny hand-cut squares of mirror that Hodges has assembled into a six by eight foot mosaic on canvas. A viewer who stands in front of its tessellated surface sees seemingly infinite reflections of him or herself (and anything in the near distance) in each little tile (each is an individual mirror). When moving across and in front of the piece, one's reflected body appears as a sinuous wave of images that resembles a school of darting fish. Upon backing up, one's image "folds" away into the reflected light.

Hodges created *As close as I can get*, 1998, in direct response to *Folding*. He had come to imagine the individual tiles that made up the mirror compositions as "blank spaces ready for something to occur." With *As close as I can get*, Hodges repeated the mirror's grid but filled each of these "blanks" with color. The piece consists of a spectrum of one-inch square Pantone color chips assembled into a large square format. Hodges randomly assembled the chips to create an undifferentiated diffusion of color. This effect causes the viewer to lose the ability to focus on and identify specific colors. The work is a visual counterpart to the optical experience of the mirror mosaic.

Hodges' photographs reference the mirror works, too, in the sense that a camera is, essentially, a series of mirrors positioned to trap light, and a photograph its paper record. The most basic function of our eyes is to gather light, yet they simultaneously record our unique views of the world around us. His photographs often have the offhand quality of snapshots; they achieve the resonance of art objects through fortuitous accident, capturing the artist's experience of a particular moment more than they document an object or event. For example, *a small ending*, 2001, would have been a straightforward recording of trees and sky—were it not for a vibrant yellow blur that appeared as part of the image because Hodges unwittingly exposed the film to light. While rarely so visible in his practice, he welcomes such random occurrences, feeling they reveal truths that would not otherwise be accessed.

His acute concentration on light as subject led Hodges to begin using actual light as a material in the form of commercial lightbulbs. These works follow a geometric order; comprising gridded rows of bulbs screwed into enameled white square or rectangular panels that house electrical hardware. The panels themselves are about two inches deep and mount flush to the wall as single units or in multipart arrangements.

In their reliance on the wall as support; their frontal presentation; and their formal consideration of light, color, shape, and form, the lightbulb pieces function like paintings. Because they project light, these works extend painting's adherence to a flat rectilinear surface. Hodges' love of color is abundantly clear in these works. He employs the full variety of commercially available colors, designs, sockets, wattages, and shapes of bulbs, enabling him to explore color relationships and blend colors. Radiating colors converge, overlap, and dissolve, and change in appearance throughout the day and as day merges into night.

Ultimate Joy, 2001, pairs two square panels hung on the diagonal to meet at their inside tips. For this piece, Hodges mostly selected bulbs of a nearly uniform, muted blue, though at the center of the composition is a group of bulbs in various bright colors, some paired in dual sockets. They appear animate, like revelers at a party. The bulbs bounce light around the room, enticing viewers to share their space. Up close to them, one's body takes on their colors—takes in their heat.

Hodges has introduced kinetic elements to several lightbulb works, such as *Just this side*, 1999. Using timers, he programmed this work's six panels of bulbs to turn on and off in a progression that approximated the passage of a day. The bottom two panels switch on at first; later they are joined by the two panels directly above, and so on. At a certain point all the lights are on. Later the first panels lit switch off. Eventually all the panels turn off. Within this complex composition each bulb's color remains distinct, yet they also blend to approximate the colors and effects of the passage of a day. Wherever the work is presented, it is synchronized to the local time zone.

One constant that runs through Hodges' practice is the play between the illusion and the literal. If *Just this side* interprets the passage of a day in electric lights, *Overlaps under there*, 1999, adapts the lightbulb sculptures into a work on paper. As its title suggests, one sees overlapping layers of colored tissue through a top sheet of white paper, whose surface has been cut with irregularly spaced holes. This piece neatly reverses the effects of the lightbulb works: the colored areas in *Overlaps under there* are confined within the white template instead of spilling out and blending upon it; also, the layered tissues within each circular frame create new colors, whereas the bulbs within the panels retain their autonomous hues.

The artist's recent Prismacolor pencil works on paper and on the wall are boldly graphic and brilliantly colored. They focus on the formal fundamentals of line, shape, and color. He creates geometric forms such as fans cropped by the edges of a paper sheet, circles within circles, and intersecting arcs. Lines often radiate out from a central point, in much the same way that light typically is represented as straight lines emanating from a single source. In the drawing, *Happy/Sunrise-Sunset*, 2001, two fans, one predominantly of sunrise lavenders/pinks, the other of sunset yellows/ oranges, converge inward and overlap to form a central

a small ending, 2001
digital print
16.5 x 22"
Collection of the artist

pointed ellipse of interwoven colors. *Happy/Sunrise-Sunset* is an exercise in simple geometry, a color study of formal sophistication, and a symbolic representation of the special harmony that can exist between two people.

Hodges' site-specific Prismacolor wall drawings engage the physical properties of a space, its architecture, and its natural and artificial light. They are subtle and modest, yet yield vivid results. In a recent exhibition at CRG Gallery in New York, Hodges created temporary wall drawings in response to the gallery's architecture and the way it changed according to the character of the natural light. At the gallery's entrance, where direct sunlight hit the wall, he drew a yellow fan shape that critic Robert Mahoney described as seeming "almost burned there by the sun itself." Farther into the space, at an exterior corner where two walls meet, Hodges drew a half circle of multicolored lines that folded around the walls in two equal arcs. For a portion of each afternoon, the sun's rays illuminated the work in such a way that it seemed to pulse with sunlight.

Again and again, Hodges demonstrates how the most humble and direct approaches can yield profound results. In light, he has discovered an elemental subject and material with multiple associative and phenomenological qualities. Hodges has a remarkable ability to engage and interconnect the full spectrum of those qualities.

Untitled (Landscape VI), 2000–2001
sheet music collage
21 x 22"
Collection of Christina and
James Lockwood

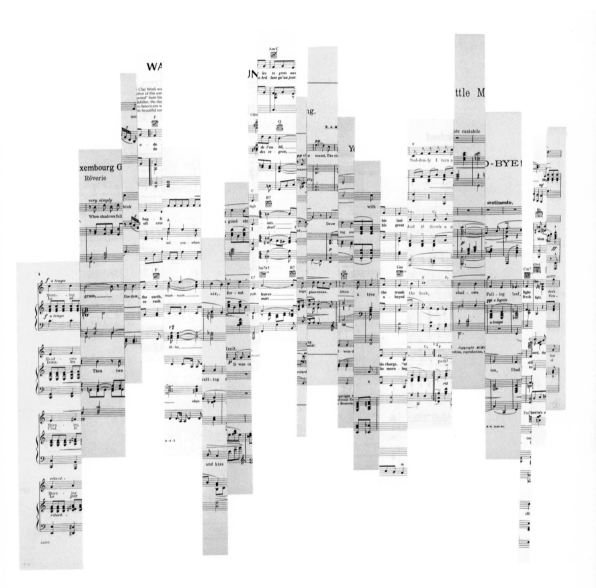

into everything, 2002
Coloraid paper with adhesive
on paper
35 x 47.5"
Collection of Nancy and
Joel Portnoy

where the sky fills in, 2002
c-print
76 x 50"
The Museum of Modern Art,
New York. Promised gift
of Agnes Gund

(pages 66–72)
The following photographs from
endlessly, 2002
Series of fouteen c-prints
Dimensions variable

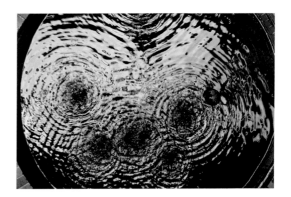

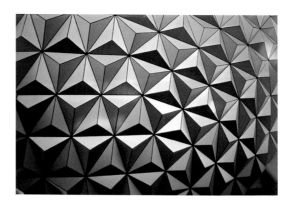

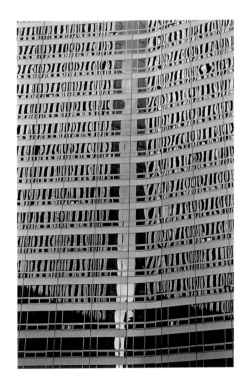

Oh Great Terrain, 2002
Latex paint
Dimensions variable
Installation view, *this and this*,
CRG Gallery, New York, 2002

(pages 76–77)
Installation view, *this and this*,
CRG Gallery, New York, 2002

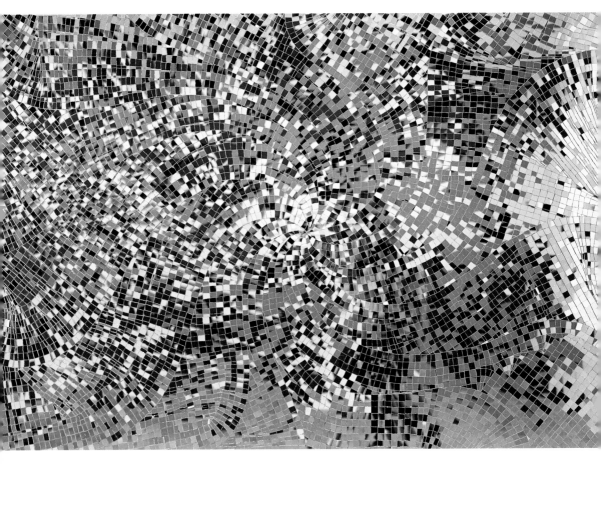

PARTS AND ALL by Allan Schwartzman

Although I got turned onto art by looking at paintings, it was often art historians who unlocked art's mysteries. Art and words are a complicated pairing. Indeed, much art is easier to verbally justify than to revere. Sometimes, even, art seems to have been created by the same verbal culture obsessed with analysis and historicization that was meant to interpret it. Conversely, some of the most compelling art can intimidate writers into neglectful submission.

Jim Hodges is just such an artist. The strengths and beauties of his work are subtle, poetic, and polyvalent. In writing this essay, I have come to feel my words do little justice to the poignancy of Hodges' art. I keep talking about the subject, never penetrating its essence. This is a good sign, however personally frustrating, and increasingly rare in contemporary art practice (one that may even sound oddly old-fashioned): art that must be made because it can be expressed in no other way.

Hodges explores the big themes with straightforward (yet beautiful) works of the most incidental of materials: his "paintings" made by reassembling hundreds of shards from broken mirrors into intricate mosaics enable viewers to contemplate the complex and multifaceted nature of self-reflection; his spider-like webs made of metal chain explore the intricacy of relationships, their ways of delicate interdependence and exquisite entrapment; his screens made of artificial flowers express life, love, and loss through a language otherwise associated with cheap sentimentality. In one of his first major "mature works," *A Diary of Flowers,* Hodges drew every day on toss-off deli napkins and in the process transformed one of the most over-examined idioms of art history—the still life—into a document of relationships, loss, memory, and memorialization.

Unraveling, 2002
mirror on canvas on
wood panel
48 x 72"
Marieluise Hessel Collection

His work is always deeply personal, and yet it is not confessional and reveals little that could specifically be identified as autobiography. In short, he explores the personal sides of identity that we all share.

In his recent exhibition at CRG Gallery, Hodges presented works that looked both inward and at the physical environment: collages, straight and reconstructed photographs, mirror pieces, and a large-scale wall painting. One of the group's most ambitious works derives from a series begun two years ago in which the artist cut old sheet music into vertical strips and reconstructed them into new compositions determined by aligning similar words from disparate songs. The themes were essentials of both music and visual art, such as love, color, and landscape. In the current work, *Picturing that day*, the largest of the series to date, in the place of words the artist added chips of Color-Aid paper randomly arranged. It is an ode to artistic cross-pollination and to an intermingling of the senses—the musical nature of art, the visual nature of music, and the color of sound. In another work, he took a large-scale photograph of a tree in fall and forced the process of defoliation by cutting into the photograph and fashioning the cuts into hundreds of leaves of flickering foliage. Both a remarkable expression of the life cycle and a realistic portrayal, the work did nothing less than simulate nature's process while also recreating for the viewer the simplest pleaure of experiencing light while looking up at a tree.

Also on view were two mirror pieces. One, entitled *Unraveling*, is composed of a glorious swirling of tiny mirror pieces which fracture the light, color, and images that they pick up in bits and pieces from the surrounding space. In another, *In a Brighter Light*, the artist cut a mirror into large V-shaped strips and attached them to the wall. In a play on the notion of negative space, the center—all wall—becomes as aggressive a part of the composition as the slashes of mirror that surround it. When looking into the piece, the shapes of mirror fragment one's image and the piece becomes a study in what it means to locate oneself in the world.

In the show's largest work, a wall-sized mural, *Oh Great Terrain*, Hodges transposed the black, white, and gray camouflage pattern

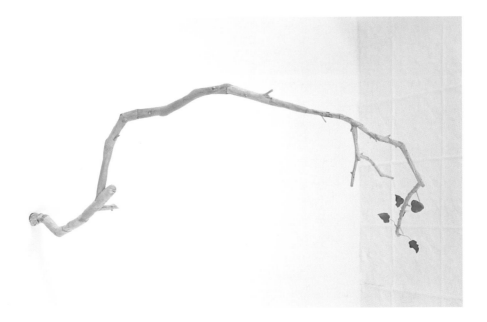

Not far, 1998
wood, glue, wire, sugar
46 x 18 x 25"
Carlos and Rosa de la Cruz
Collection

of the pants he often wears into a kaleidoscopic miasma of obfus-
cation and transformation. In *endlessly*, dotted throughout the
exhibition, photographs of various details of the experienced world
together formed a kind of scrapbook of the ordinary momentary
glimpses in which the artist sees the extraordinary: flowers, a chan-
delier, a tree, rain falling on water, a piece of lace, landscapes, and
details of urban architecture. The works were installed at heights
that suggest how they would be experienced in the real world.

Together, the works in various media were the artist's version of
"playing the standards." In their different ways, each work explored
perception, how when color, light and form fracture into hundreds
of pieces or moments or moods, they form new wholes or full
experiences.

Hodges came of age as an artist in the early 1990s, after the
brash chest-thumping of mural-size neo-expressionist painting
was decimated by an art-market crash, and after the free-for-all
exuberance and sexual exaltation of a self-liberated youth culture
were obliterated by the devastation of AIDS; when on the one hand
the supply-side Julian Schnabels and Anselm Kiefers were deemed
self-indulgent, and, more stingingly, on the other, the Keith Harings

and Robert Mapplethorpes were brought to an abrupt end by death. What emerged from the rubble of years of mourning was a paradigmatic shift in art toward issues of identity and mortality, with artists like Robert Gober and Felix Gonzalez-Torres as the reigning spirits. A shattered sense of self and the fleeting nature of time were explored in a multitude of ways. Paintings and sculptures of body parts, drawings about loss, photographs of the bits and pieces of life came to dominate art.

Amid the rage of thwarted dreams and youth silenced, new voices rose up in the early 90's. Hodges' was one of them. Hodges still examines the fragment. It was to be found everywhere in his recent show. Indeed, he has come to celebrate it, to find in it not tragedy, but a new sense of love, of what it means to be complete. In the spliced music, Hodges finds a new and colorful song, just as he casts the tree in a different stage of life in a constructed pictorial world, and in the broken mirror he fractures pictorial illusionism in order to examine a new image of self integrated into its environment according to a different perceptual reality.

Throughout the twentieth century artists tested the limits of art in all sorts of ways, even challenging its very relevance. But no one could kill it. Even Ad Reinhardt, the best of the painters of "the last painting," couldn't stop. He kept making that last painting over and over again as proof that the endgame had no end. And Andy Warhol, who could have been seen as the eulogizer of high art, in the end, cared deeply about making transcendent paintings. But today, testing the limits of art seems, pardon the expression, to have outlived its usefulness.

Art for Hodges has become a gift, an opportunity to express the joy of experience, beauty, and regeneration. Hodges confronts the fragmentation that is at the center of the post-modern sense of self and finds in it consolation, a new sense of completeness, of being whole. His art celebrates a kind of survival that is maturity and discovers the poetry in it—parts and all.

everything will happen, 2003
c-print
72 x 48"
Carlos and Rosa de la Cruz Collection

See I, 2003
mirror on aluminum
60 x 80"
Private Collection, London

(overleaf:)
Untitled (Love), 2000–2001
sheet music collage
26.75 x 39"
Whitney Museum of American Art,
New York; purchase, with funds
from Faith Golding Linden 2002.199

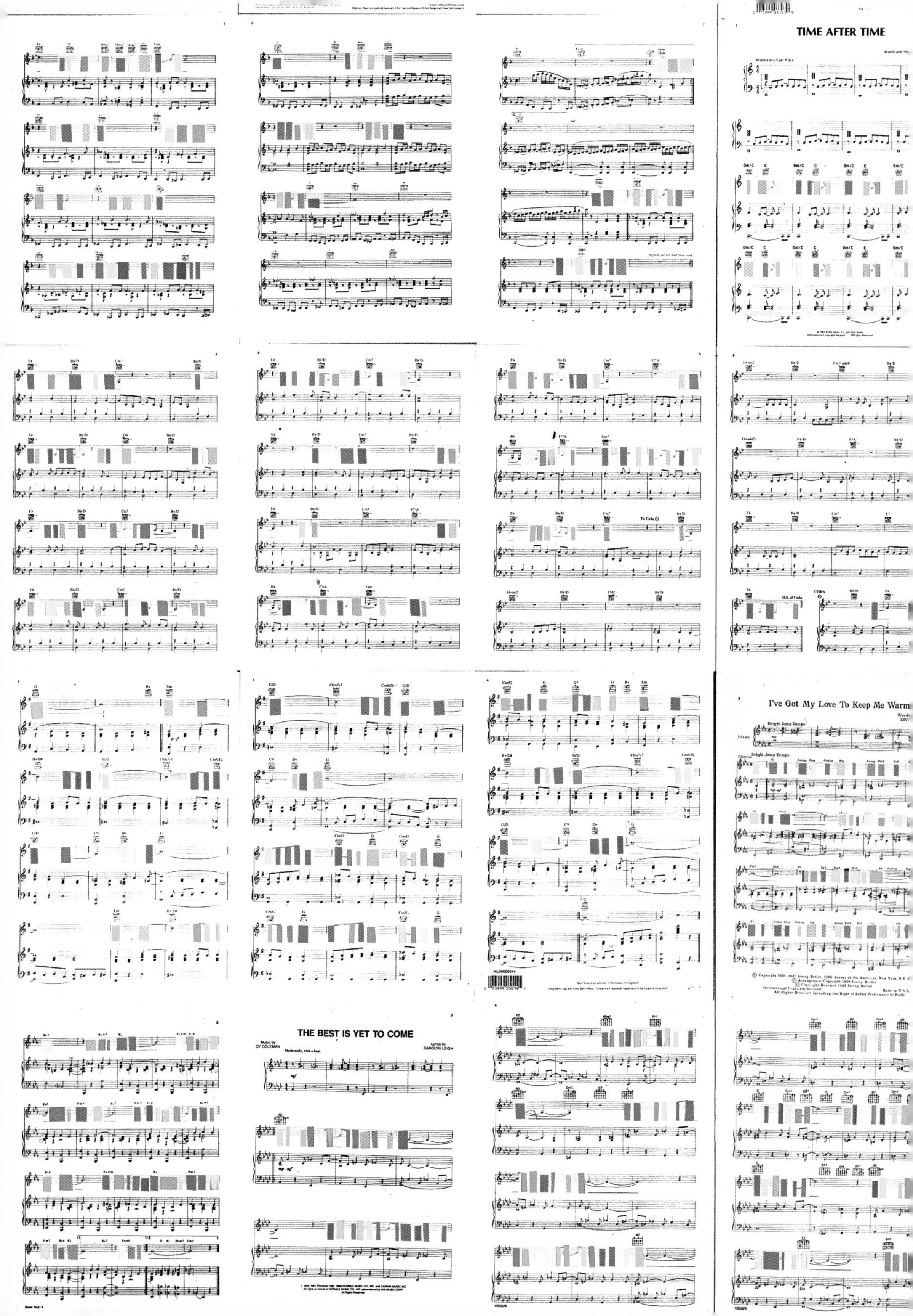

TIME AFTER TIME
Moderately Fast Rock
To Coda
D.S. al Coda
CODA
I've Got My Love To Keep Me Warm
Bright Jump Tempo
THE BEST IS YET TO COME
Music by
CY COLEMAN
Lyrics by
CAROLYN LEIGH
Moderately, with a beat
HL00005014

Picturing that day, 2002
(detail)
sheet music collage
84 x 72"
Courtesy of the artist and
CRG Gallery, New York

89

Corridor, 2003
The bells, 2002 (in back)
latex paint, glass, wood, and rope
Dimensions variable
Courtesy of the artist and
CRG Gallery, New York
Installation view, *colorsound*,
Addison Gallery of American Art,
Phillips Academy, Andover,
Massachusetts, 2003

Slower than this, 2001
cut photograph on paper
66 x 30"
Courtesy of the artist and
Stephen Friedman Gallery,
London

IT WAS A RAINY NIGHT.
IT WAS A WARM WIND
MORNING IN SPRING.
IT WAS A MOUNTAIN TOP
THE SNOW WAS BEGINNING
TO MELT.
IT WAS A SLOW SUNSET.
IT WAS L.A.
IT WAS EARLY AFTERNOON.
IT WAS RAINING.
IT HAD STARTED TO RAIN.
IT WAS A LONG TIME AGO.
IT WAS QUIET AND DARK.
IT WAS HAPPENING
ALL AROUND US.
IT HAD STARTED EARLIER
THAT DAY.
IT HAD DEVELOPED
OVER TIME.
IT HAD BEGUN LIKE ANY
OTHER DAY.

IT WAS WITH THE PASSING
OF A SINGLE BIRD
FROM TREE TO WIRE.
IT WAS SO WARM.
IT WAS LONG AGO.

IT WAS BUILDING AND
COULDN'T BE KEPT DOWN.
IT HAD STARTED A LONG
TIME AGO.
IT HAD TO HAPPEN.
IT COULDN'T BE STOPPED.
IT WAS AS IF IT WASN'T
HAPPENING.
IT WAS A BLANK SPACE,
A BLACK OUT- THE SEA-
THE SOUND OF WAVES -
ENDLESS MOTION. IT WAS
THE EARTH BREATHING,
THE SOUND OF AIR -
THE PASSING CAR -
THE TRAFFIC.
IT HAD STARTED
LIKE ANY OTHER DAY.

Study for A view from in there, 2003
graphite and colored pencil on paper
22 x 30"
Collection of David Willis

(facing page)
A view from in there, 2003
glass
7 x 5.5 x 25.5"
Courtesy of the artist and
Stephen Freidman Gallery, London

1. *stay close*, 1995
pre-stretched, pre-primed canvases,
steel bolts
120 x 120 x 60
Courtesy of the artist and
CRG Gallery, New York

2. *on we go*, 1996
metal chain with pins
57 x 48 x 22
Collection of Eileen and
Peter Norton, Santa Monica

3. *With the wind*, 1997
scarves, thread
90 x 99 x 5
Collection of Penny Cooper
and Rena Rosenwasser

4. *As close as I can get*, 1998
Pantone color chips with
adhesive tape
81 x 81
Collection of Eileen and
Peter Norton, Santa Monica

5. *Folding (into a greater world)*, 1998
mirror on canvas
72 x 96
Collection of Eileen and
Peter Norton, Santa Monica

6. *Overlaps under there*, 1999
tissue paper with cut paper
30 x 22.5
Private Collection, New York

7. *Corridor*, 1999
Prismacolor on paper
22 x 30
Collection of Javier and
Monica G. Mora, Coral Gables

8. *this (from ordinary life)*, 1999
mirror with motor
22 x 16 x 1
Collection of Eileen and
Peter Norton, Santa Monica

10. *With*, 1999
lightbulbs, ceramic sockets,
wood and metal panels
31.5 x 63 x 5
Private Collection, New York

11. *Coming through*, 1999
lightbulbs, ceramic sockets,
wood and metal panels
31.5 x 63 x 5
Collection of Rebecca and
Alexander Stewart, Seattle

12. *Just this side*, 1999
(Weatherspoon only)
lightbulbs, ceramic sockets,
wood and metal panels
45 x 22.5
Collection of Howard and
Donna Stone

13. *Ahhhh*, 2000
lightbulbs, ceramic sockets,
wood and metal panels
45 x 35 x 20
Marieluise Hessel Collection on
permanent loan to the Center for
Curatorial Studies, Bard College,
Annadale-on-Hudson, New York

14. *Ultimate Joy* , 2001
lightbulbs, ceramic and plastic
sockets, wood and metal panels
32 x 64 x 9
Collection of Linda Pace

15. *a small ending*, 2001
digital print
16.5 x 22
Collection of the artist

16. *Oh, forever*, 2001
aluminum foil on paper
47.25 x 35
Collection of Nancy and
Steven Oliver

17. *Happy/Sunrise-Sunset ("In the
Beginning is My End"– T.S. Eliot)*,
2001
Prismacolor on paper
47.5 x 35
Private Collection

18. *Untitled (Landscape VI)*,
2000–2001
sheet music collage
21 x 22
Collection of Christina and
James Lockwood

19. *Untitled (near and far)*, 2002
(Tang only)
mirror on Aluqua bond
78 x 81
Collection of Marlene and
David Persky

20. *into everything*, 2002 (Tang only)
Coloraid paper with adhesive
on paper
35 x 47.5
Collection of Nancy and Joel Portnoy

21. *where the sky fills in*, 2002
(Tang only)
c-print
76 x 50
The Museum of Modern Art, New
York. Promised gift of Agnes Gund

22. *everything will happen*, 2003
(Weatherspoon only)
c-print
72 x 48
Carlos and Rosa de la Cruz
Collection

23. *Oh Great Terrain, (White)*, 2003
Latex paint
Dimensions variable
Courtesy of the artist and CRG
Gallery, New York
(at each venue the artist will create
wall works specific to the space)

stay close, 1995
230 pre-stretched, pre-primed
canvases, steel bolts
120 x 120 x 60"
Courtesy of the artist and
CRG Gallery, New York
Installation view, Tang Museum,
Skidmore College, 2003

100

images from the series,
Our Simple Selves, 1995

JIM HODGES

Born in Spokane, Washington in 1957
Lives and works in New York, New York

Education

1986 Master of Fine Arts, Pratt Institute, Brooklyn, New York
1980 Bachelor of Fine Arts, Fort Wright College, Spokane, Washington

Solo Exhibitions

(Exhibitions are followed by dates where available. Traveling exhibitions are
listed under their initial date and venue)

2003

Jim Hodges, The Tang Teaching Museum and Art Gallery, Skidmore College,
  Saratoga Springs, New York, June 21–August 31; Austin Museum of Art,
  Austin, Texas, February 21–May 23, 2004; Weatherspoon Art Museum,
  University of North Carolina, Greensboro, North Carolina, August 8–
  October 24, 2004, Museum of Contemporary Art Cleveland, Cleveland, Ohio,
  January 27–May 1, 2005
Jim Hodges, Stephen Friedman Gallery, London, England, June 10–July 26
colorsound, Addison Gallery of American Art, Phillips Academy, Andover,
  Massachusetts, April 12–July 31
Returning, ArtPace, San Antonio, Texas, January 9–April 6

2002

this and this, CRG Gallery, New York, September 9–June 22
Jim Hodges: Constellation of an Ordinary Day, Jundt Art Museum,
  Gonzaga University, Spokane, Washington, September 2–November 2
Jim Hodges: Subway Music Box, Northwest Museum of Arts & Culture,
  Spokane, Washington, July 25–November 3; Eastern Washington State
  Historical Society/Cheney Cowle Museum, Spokane, Washington
like this, Dieu Donné Papermill, New York, April 24–June 1

2001

Jim Hodges, Galeria Camargo Vilaça, São Paulo, Brazil, December

2000

Jim Hodges, Anthony Meier Fine Arts, San Francisco, May 5–June 9
Capp Street Project: Jim Hodges: Subway Music Box, Oliver Art Center,
  California College of Arts and Crafts, Oakland, California, April 15–May 6

1999

Jim Hodges, Miami Art Museum, Miami, October 22, 1999–January 9, 2000
Jim Hodges: every way, Museum of Contemporary Art, Chicago, January
  16–April 11; Institute of Contemporary Art, Boston, September 8–October 1
Jim Hodges, Marc Foxx Gallery, Los Angeles, May 28–June 19

1998

Jim Hodges, CRG Gallery, New York, September 11–October 10

Jim Hodges: Welcome, The Kemper Museum of Contemporary Art,
Kansas City, Missouri, April 9–June 14

1997

Jim Hodges: No Betweens and More, Site Santa Fe, Santa Fe, New Mexico,
March 15–June 22

Jim Hodges, Galerie Ghislaine Hussenot, Paris, France

1996

States, The Fabric Workshop and Museum, Philadelphia, Pennsylvania,
April 25–June 15

yes, Marc Foxx, Santa Monica, California

Nothing, 1993
white brass chain in closet
96 x 48 x 36"
Installation view, Paul Morris,
New York

1995

Jim Hodges, CRG Gallery, New York, October 28–December 9

Jim Hodges, Center for Curatorial Studies, Bard College, Annandale-on-Hudson,
New York, September 23–December 2

1994

Jim Hodges: A Diary of Flowers, CRG Gallery,
New York, January 7–February 26

Everything For You, Interim Art, London, England

1992

New Aids Drug, Het Apollohuis, Eindhoven, Holland

1991

White Room, White Columns, New York,
December 13, 1991–January 13, 1992

1989

Historia Abscondita, Ad Gallery, Gonzaga University,
Spokane, Washington, October 6–October 27

1986

Master of Fine Arts Thesis Exhibition, Pratt Institute,
New York

Selected Group Exhibitions

2003

Site and Insight, P.S.1 Contemporary Art Center, Long Island City, New York,
June 29–August 31

New Material as New Media: The Fabric Workshop and Museum at 25 Years,
The Fabric Workshop and Museum, Philadelphia, Pennsylvania,
February 10–April 19

2002

Mirror Mirror, Massachusetts Museum of Contemporary Art, North Adams,
Massachusetts, October 5–January 5, 2003

Miami Currents: Linking Collection and Community, Miami Art Museum,
Miami, October 30–March 2, 2003

Life Death Love Hate Pleasure Pain, Museum of Contemporary Art, Chicago,
October 19–January 19, 2003

Arte Povera American Style: Funk, Play, Poetry & Labor, Reinberger Galleries,
The Cleveland Institute of Art, Cleveland, October 18–December 18

de Kooning to Today: Highlights from the Permanent Collection,
Whitney Museum of American Art, New York,
October 17–November 2, 2003

Mask or Mirror? A Play of Portraits, Worcester Museum of Art,
Worcester, Massachusetts, October 6, 2002–January 26, 2003

Chapter V, Art Resources Transfer, New York, August 1–August 23

All the Way with Jim + Shel, Jim Hodges and Shelley Hirsch,
Portland Institute for Contemporary Art, Portland, Oregon,
June 26–August 24

Linger, Artemis Greenberg Van Doren Gallery, New York,
June 13–July 26

Pretty, ATM Gallery, New York, May 10–June 12

Summer Group Exhibition, Marc Foxx Gallery, Los Angeles

2001

Patterns: Between Object and Arabesque, Kunsthallen Brandts
Klædefabrik, Odense, Denmark, September 22–December 21

CAMERA WORKS: The Photographic Impulse in Contemporary Art,
Marianne Boesky Gallery, New York, June 28–August 10

Uncommon Threads: Contemporary Artists and Clothing, Herbert F.
Johnson Museum of Art, Cornell University, Ithaca, New York,
March 17–June 17

2000

Of the Moment: Contemporary Art from the Permanent Collection,
San Francisco Museum of Modern Art, San Francisco,
June 30–August 29

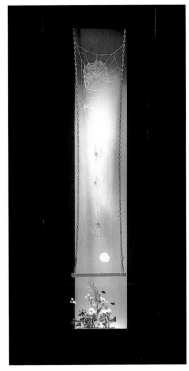

Our perfect world, 1993 (detail)
mixed media installation
Dimensions variable
Installation view, Grey Art
Gallery, New York

Gardens of Pleasure, John Michael Kohler Arts Center, Sheboygan, Wisconsin,
    June 11–September 17
Projects 70—Jim Hodges, Beatriz Milhazes, Faith Ringgold, Museum of Modern
    Art, New York, May 1–October 31
Age of Influence: Reflections in the Mirror of American Culture, Museum
    of Contemporary Art, Chicago, April 8–January 7
Vanitas: Meditations on Life and Death in Contemporary Art, Virginia Museum
    of Fine Arts, Richmond, Virginia, April 4–June 18
Outbound: Passages from the 90's, Contemporary Arts Museum, Houston,
    Texas, March 4–May 7
et comme l'esperance est violente.., Frac des Pays de la Loire, Carquefou, France
The Trunk Show, Zoller Gallery, Penn State University, University Park,
    Pennsylvania
*ZONA F: An approach to the spaces inhabited by the feminist discourses
    in contemporary art*, Espai d'Art Contemporani de Castelló, Castelló, Spain

1999

1999 Drawings, Alexander and Bonin, New York, December 11–January 22, 2000
Natural Dependency, Jerwood Gallery, London, England,
    November 3– December 12
Regarding Beauty: A View of the Late 20th Century, Hirshhorn Museum and
    Sculpture Garden, Washington, D.C., October 7–January 17, 2000;
    Haus der Kunst, Munich, Germany, February 11, 2000–April 30, 2000
The American Century: Art and Culture, Part II, 1950–2000, The Whitney
    Museum of American Art, New York, September 26–February 13, 2000
*Matter of Time: Jim Hodges, Charles LeDray, Michelle Segre, and
    Jonathan Seliger*, Dorsky Gallery, New York, September 7–October 23
Not There, Rena Bransten Gallery, June 10–July 10
Collectors Collect Contemporary: 1990-1999, Institute of Contemporary Art,
    Boston, March 31–May 29
Flowers on Fabric: Flora and Friends , The Fabric Workshop and Museum,
    Philadelphia , Pennsylvania, February 25–June, 2000
Fresh Flowers, Bellevue Art Museum, Bellevue, Washington, January 30–April 4

1998

Abstract Painting, Once Removed, Contemporary Arts Museum, Houston, Texas,
    October 3–December 6; Kemper Museum of Contemporary Art, Kansas City,
    Missouri, April 23–July 18, 1999
Let Freedom Ring, Institute of Contemporary Art Boston,
    September 10– September 29
Political Pictures: Confrontation and Commemoration in Recent Art, Robert
    Hull Fleming Museum, University of Vermont, Burlington, Vermont,
    September 8–November 13
AIDS WORLDS—Between Resignation and Hope, Centre d'Art Contemporain,
    Geneva, Switzerland

1997

Present Tense: Nine Artists in the Nineties, San Francisco Museum of Modern
Art, San Francisco, September 13–January 13, 1998

Contemporary Projects: Longing and Memory, Los Angeles County Museum
of Art, Los Angeles, June 5–September 8

Gothic: Transmutations of Horror in Late Twentieth Century Art, Institute
of Contemporary Art, Boston, April 24–July 6

7th Bienal Internacional de Esculturae Desenho das Caldas da Rainha Bienal,
Portugal

Des Fleurs en Mai, FRAC, Nantes, France

Hanging by a Thread, Hudson River Museum, Yonkers, New York

Poetics of Obsession, Linda Kirkland Gallery, New York

1996

UNIVERSALIS, The 23rd International São Paulo Bienal, São Paulo, Brazil,
October 5–December 8

Just Past: The Contemporary in MOCA's Permanent Collection 1975–1996,
Museum of Contemporary Art, Los Angeles, September 29–January 19, 1997

Masculine Measures, John Michael Kohler Arts Center, Sheboygan, Wisconsin,
January 28–May 12

Material Matters, A.O.I. Gallery, Santa Fe, New Mexico

Swag & Puddle, The Work Space, New York

Title, Galerie Ghislaine Hussenot, Paris, France

One with the other, 1998
white cedar
Dimensions variable
Installation view,
MCA Chicago
Private Collection, New York

1995

Avant-Garde Walk a Venezia, Venice Biennale, Venice,
Italy, June 1995

soucis de pensées, Art: Concept/Olivier Antoine, Nice,
France, March 10–April 21

Material Dreams, Gallery Takashimaya, New York,
January 14–March 11

*In a Different Light Visual Culture, Sexual Identity,
Queer Practice*, University Art Museum, Berkeley,
California, January 11–April 9

Late Spring, Marc Foxx, Los Angeles

Mon Voyage à New York, Galerie Elizabeth Valleix,
Paris, France

New Works, Feigen Gallery, Chicago

1994

It's how you play the game, Exit Art/The First World,
New York, November 5–January 28, 1995

Ethereal Materialism, Apex Art, New York,
October 15–November 26

Les fleurs de mon jardin, Galerie Alain Gutharc, Paris, France,
    September 10–October 20
The Garden, Barbara Krakow Gallery, Boston, March 12–April 6
DYAD, Williamsburg, Brooklyn, New York

1993
Our Perfect World, Grey Art Gallery, New York, September 14–October 30
The Art of Self Defense and Revenge...It's Really Hard, Momenta Art,
    New York, May 1–May 29
Paper Trails: The Eidetic Image: Contemporary American Works on Paper,
    Krannert Art Museum, University of Illinois at Urbana-Champaign, Illinois,
    March 17–April 18
Beyond Attrition: Art in the Era of Aids, Washington Project for the Arts,
    Washington, D.C.
Jim Hodges and Bill Jacobson, Paul Morris Fine Art, New York
Museo Statale d'Arte Mediovale e Moderna, Arezzo, Italy
Outside Possibilities, The Rushmore Festival, Woodbury, New York
Sculpture & Multiples, Brooke Alexander, New York
Selections/Spring '93, The Drawing Center, New York

Oh Great Terrain, (White), 2003
latex paint
Dimensions variable
Installation view, Tang
Museum, Skidmore College
Courtesy of the artist and
CRG Gallery, New York

1992

Collector's Show, Arkansas Arts Center, Little Rock, Arkansas,
    December 3–December 27
Healing, Rena Bransten Gallery, San Francisco, California, May 12–June 13
An Ode to Gardens and Flowers, Nassau County Museum of Art, Roslyn Harbor,
    New York
Update 1992, White Columns, New York

1991

Black and White, Nancy Hoffman Gallery, New York, June 7–September 3
Lyric, Uses of Beauty at the End of the Century, White Columns, New York

1990

Jim Hodges, David Nyzio, Vincent Shine, Postmasters, New York
Reclamation, Momenta Art Alternatives, Philadelphia

1988

Selections from the Artists File, Artist's Space, New York,
    November 17–January 7, 1989
Installation, Momenta Art Alternatives, Philadelphia

Audience view, Jim Hodges
lecture, Whitney Museum of
American Art, New York, 2000

Bibliography

Selected Books, Catalogues, and Brochures

Abstract Painting, Once Removed. Exhibition catalogue. Houston:
Contemporary Arts Museum, 1998. Essay by Dana Friis-Hansen.

Arte Povera American Style: Funk, Play, Poetry & Labor. Exhibition catalogue.
Cleveland: Cleveland Institute of Art, 2002. Introduction by Bruce Checefsky
and Julie Langsam.

Avant-garde walk a Venezia: 8–12 juin 1995. Exhibition catalogue.
Venice: Edizioni d'arte fratelli Pozzo, 1995.

Benezra, Neal David, Olga M. Viso, and Arthur C. Danto. *Regarding Beauty:
A View of the Late 20th Century*. Exhibition catalogue. Washington D.C. and
Ostfildern, Germany: Hirshhorn Museum and Sculpture Garden and Cantz
Publishers, 1999.

Bishop, Janet C, Gary Garrels, and John S. Weber. *Present Tense: Nine Artists
in the Nineties: Janet Cardiff, Iran do Espírito Santo, Felix Gonzalez-Torres,
Jim Hodges, Charles LeDray, Gabriel Orozco, Jennifer Pastor, Kathryn Spence,
Steve Wolfe*. Exhibition catalogue. San Francisco: San Francisco Museum
of Modern Art, 1997.

Blake, Nayland, Lawrence Rinder, and Amy Scholder, eds. *In a Different Light:
Visual Culture, Sexual Identity, Queer Practice*. Exhibition catalogue.
San Francisco: City Lights Books, 1995.

Capp Street Project: Jim Hodges Subway Music Box. Exhibition brochure.
Oakland, California: Oliver Art Center at California College of Arts and
Crafts, 2000. Interview with Lawrence Rinder.

Contemporary Projects 1: Longing and Memory. Exhibition brochure.
Los Angeles: Los Angeles County Museum of Art, 1997. Essay by Lynn
Zelevansky.

Friis-Hansen, Dana, Lynn M. Herbert, Marti Mayo, and Paola Morsiani.
Outbound: Passages from the 90's. Exhibition catalogue. Houston:
Contemporary Arts Museum, 2000.

Grunenberg, Christoph, ed. *Gothic: Transmutations of Horror in Late Twentieth
Century Art*. Exhibition catalogue. Cambridge, Mass.: ICA Boston and MIT
Press, 1997.

Jim Hodges. Artist book. New York: CRG Gallery, 1995. Essay by Julie Ault.

Jim Hodges. Exhibition brochure. São Paulo: Galeria Camargo Vilaça, 2001.

Jim Hodges: every way. Exhibition catalogue. Chicago: Museum of
Contemporary Art, 1999. Essay by Amada Cruz.

Jim Hodges: No Betweens and More. Exhibition brochure. Santa Fe: SITE
Santa Fe, 1997.

Jim Hodges: Welcome. Exhibition brochure. Kansas City, Missouri:
Kemper Museum of Contemporary Art, 1998. Essay by Dana Self.

Untitled, 2000
silk scarves, newspaper,
cardboard boxes, and thread
Dimensions variable
Stage set for T*ell Me the Truth
About Love*
Collaboration with
Tom Bogdan and Terry Creach
Installation view, St. Marks
Church, New York

Mask or Mirror? A Play of Portraits. Worcester, Massachusetts: Worcester Art
Museum, 2002. Essay by Susan Stoops.

Material Dreams. Exhibition catalogue. New York: The Gallery at Takashimaya
with the cooperation of the Fabric Workshop, 1995. Essay by Lynn Gumpert.

*Matter of Time: Jim Hodges, Charles LeDray, Michelle Segre, and Jonathan
Seliger.* Exhibition brochure. New York: Dorsky Gallery, 1999.

Morgan, Jessica. *Collectors Collect Contemporary Art: 1990–99.*
Exhibition catalogue. Boston: The Institute of Contemporary Art, 1999.

Phillips, Lisa. *The American Century: Art & Culture 1950–2000.*
Exhibition catalogue. New York: Whitney Museum of American Art
in association with W.W. Norton & Co., 1999.

Political Pictures: Confrontation and Commemoration in Recent Art.
Exhibition catalogue. Burlington, Vermont: Robert Hull Fleming Museum,
University of Vermont, 1998.

Projects 70: Jim Hodges, Beatriz Milhazes, Faith Ringgold. Exhibition brochure.
New York: Museum of Modern Art, 1999. Essay by Fereshteh Daftari.

Selections from the Artists File. Exhibition catalogue. New York: Artist's Space,
1988. Notes by Valerie Smith.

Stroud, Marion Boulton. *New Material as New Media.* Cambridge,
Massachusetts and London, England: MIT Press, 2003

Ulmer, Sean M. *Uncommon Threads:
Contemporary Artists and Clothing.* Exhibition
catalogue. Ithaca, New York: Herbert F. Johnson
Museum of Art, Cornell University, 2001.

UNIVERSALIS: 23 Bienal Internacional São Paulo.
Exhibition catalogue. São Paulo: Fundação
Bienal de São Paulo, 1996. Essay by Paul
Schimmel. In English and Portuguese.

Overlaps under there, 1999
tissue paper with cut paper
30 x 22.5"
Private Collection, New York

Untitled, 2001
Prismacolor on wall
Dimensions variable
Installation view,
CRG Gallery, New York

Selected Articles and Reviews

Arning, Bill. "Jim Hodges: An Artist's Mirror Image." *OUT* 58 (September 1998): 38.

Baker, Kenneth. "Musical Gifts from Underground." Review. *San Francisco Chronicle* (22 April 2000): E1.

Benjamin, Marina. "One Sensation after Another." Review. *Evening Standard* (5 November 1999): 62.

Brown, Glen R. "Jim Hodges: Kemper Museum of Contemporary Art." Review. *New Art Examiner* 26, no 1 (September 1998): 46.

Canning, Susan M. "Ethereal Materialism." Review. *New Art Examiner* 22 (February 1995): 43–44.

Clemmer, David. "SITE Santa Fe, Santa Fe, New Mexico." Review. *Flash Art,* no 195 (Summer 1997): 98.

Cotter, Holland. "Art Review: Messages Woven, Sewn or Floating in the Air." Review. *The New York Times* (9 January 1998): E37.

_____."Art in Review: Jim Hodges." Review. *The New York Times* (25 September 1998): E35.

Darling, Michael. "Review: Longing and Memory." Review. *LA Weekly* (20–26 June 1997)

Decter, Joshua. "Jim Hodges." Review. *Artforum* 35, no 3 (November 1996): 104–105.

Deitcher, David. "Death in the Marketplace." *Frieze* 29 (June/July/August 1996): 140–145.

Dobrzynski, Judith H. "Taking the Ordinary and Finding the Beautiful." *The New York Times* (24 March 1999): E1.

Subway Music Box, 2000
video projection with sound
Dimensions variable
Installation view, CCAC
Institute/Oliver Art Center,
Oakland, California

Harris, Susan. "Jim Hodges: CRG." Review. *Artnews* 93, no 4 (April 1994): 173.

____. "Jim Hodges at CRG." Review. *Art in America* 91, no 1 (January 2003): 107.

Hart, Jane. "Eve Andreé Laramée, Jim Hodges." Review. *Zing Magazine* 3 (Autumn/Winter 1996/1997).

Heartney, Eleanor. "New York: Jim Hodges at CRG." Review. *Art in America* 26, no 5 (November 1998): 135.

Hegarty, Laurence. "Jim Hodges: CRG Gallery." Review. *New Art Examiner* 26, no 5 (February 1999): 54.

Horodner, Stuart. "Jim Hodges." *Bomb Magazine*, no 79 (Spring 2002): 100–101.

Hughes, Robert J. "All the Way with Jim and Shell." Review. *The Wall Street Journal* (2 August 2002): W2.

"Jim Hodges." *Art On Paper* 6, no 6 (July–August 2002): 44–45.

Johnson, Ken. "Art in Review: Jim Hodges." Review. *The New York Times* (31 May 2002): E39.

Jowitt, Deborah. "What Price Love?" *The Village Voice* (29 February 2000): 67.

____. "Slow down!" *The Village Voice* (12 November 2002): 61.

Kandel, Susan. "Review." *Los Angeles Times* (6 June 1996).

Kastner, Jeffrey. "Jim Hodges: CRG Gallery, New York." Review. *Art/Text*, no 64 (February–April 1999): 96–97.

Keats, Jonathon. "Letters to a Young Artist." *San Francisco Magazine* (February 2000): 56–57.

Killam, Brad. "Masculine Measures." Review. *New Art Examiner* 24 (September 1996): 49.

Knight, Christopher. "The Exhibition: Beguiled by Longing and Memory." Review. *The Los Angeles Times* (7 June 1997): F1.

Labelle, Charles. "Review." *Frieze* (September–October 2000): 119–120.

Levin, Kim. "Voice Choices." *The Village Voice* (28 November 1995): S1.

____. "Short List." *The Village Voice* (7 August 2001).

Mahoney, Robert. "Jim Hodges." Review. *Time Out New York* 307 (9–16 August 2001).

McClure, Lissa. "Review." *Review* (1 February 1997).

Moreno, Gean. "Interview: Jim Hodges." *New Art Examiner* 27, no 9 (June 2000): 13–15.

Perchuk, Andrew. "Jim Hodges: CRG Gallery." Review. *Artforum* 37, no 4 (December 1998): 131–132.

Rugoff, Ralph. "Beauty Bites Back." *Harper's Bazaar* (October 1999): 234–237.

Smith, Roberta. "Jim Hodges." Review. *The New York Times* (11 February 1994): C36.

____. "Critics' Choice." Review. *The New York Times* (24 November 1995).

Spector, Nancy. "Peripheral Visions: Jim Hodges and Siobhan Liddell." *The Guggenheim Magazine* (Fall 1996): 33

Temin, Christine. "Thurber, Hodges Limn a Landscape of Loss." Review. *The Boston Globe* (10 September 1999): F1.

Upshaw, Reagan. "Review of Exhibitions: Jim Hodges." Review. *Art In America* 82, no 5 (May 1994): 109–110.

Weinstein, Matthew. "New York: Jim Hodges." Review. *Artforum* 32, no 9 (May 1994): 102.

"Working Proof." *Art on Paper* 3, no. 6 (July/August 1999): 50–54.

Another Turn, 1999
Where are we now?, 1999
(in back)
Installation view, *Jim Hodges*,
Miami Art Museum, 1999

ACKNOWLEDGEMENTS

This project celebrates the art of Jim Hodges with a group of twenty works from 1995 to 2003—the largest museum exhibition of his artwork to date. We have both been inspired by Jim's work for many years and are delighted to present this exhibition as the first collaboration between our two institutions. We would first like to thank Nancy Doll, Director, Weatherspoon Art Museum, and Charles Stainback, Dayton Director, Tang Teaching Museum and Art Gallery, for their wholehearted support of this project. We are pleased and honored that the Museum of Contemporary Art in Cleveland and the Austin Museum of Art in Austin, Texas will participate in the exhibition's tour, and thank Margo Crutchfield, Curator and Jill Snyder, Director at MOCA, and Dana Friis-Hansen, Executive Director at Austin, for their support.

Jim Hodges' work is often delicate and fragile, and we are most grateful to the following individuals and institutions who allowed us to borrow works for this exhibition: Penny Cooper and Rena Rosenwasser; Carlos and Rosa de la Cruz; The Marieluise Hessel Collection on permanent loan to the Center for Curatorial Studies at Bard College; Christina and James Lockwood; Javier and Monica G. Mora; The Museum of Modern Art, New York; Agnes Gund; the Collection of Eileen and Peter Norton; Nancy and Steven Oliver; Linda Pace; Marlene and David Persky; Nancy and Joel Portnoy; Rebecca and Alexander Stewart; Howard and Donna Stone; CRG Gallery; and several private collectors.

At the Tang Museum, thanks to the funders of the Opener series, the Laurie Tisch Sussman Foundation, The New York State Council on the Arts, the Overbrook Foundation, and the Friends of the Tang.

This catalogue demonstrates the inspired work of graphic designer Bethany Johns, who has sensitively crafted this book, with photographs by Zindman–Fremont, Frank Graham, and Arthur Evans. We express our gratitude to Allan Schwartzman for his insightful essay, and CRG Gallery, and Carlos and Rosa de la Cruz for their generous support of the publication.

Carla Chammas, Richard Desroche, and Glenn McMillan of CRG Gallery in New York have been ever-present partners during the organization of all facets of this project. They answered innumerable questions, assisted with loans and catalogue details, and provided steady encouragement throughout. Also at CRG, thanks to Brian Monte, Glen Baldridge, and Alex Dodge for their critical support. Thanks to Louise Hunnicut who expertly assisted with the fabrication of wall paintings, Gretchen Bennet, at Jim Hodges' studio, who was a consistent help, and Adam Weinberg, Ann Schaffer, Marcia Acita, and Kay Newell for their assistance.

At the Tang Museum, thanks to installation crew members Sam Coe, Torrance Fish, Jefferson Nelson, Chris Oliver, Patrick O'Rourke, Alex Roediger, Pearl Rucker, Thaddeus Smith, and Joe Yetto. Thanks to Tang staff Tyler Auwarter, Helaina Blume, Jill Cohan, Ginger Ertz, Jill Handford, Lori Geraghty, Elizabeth Karp, Susi Kerr, Gayle King, Chris Kobuskie, Barbara Schrade, and Gretchen Wagner. Also thanks to Elizabeth Laub, Barbara Melville, Mary Jo Driscoll, and Barry Pritzker for their support, and museum interns Rosie Garschina, Megan Hurst, Kristen Carbone, Ellie Forseter, Eizabeth Low, Jason Lombardi, Fitzhugh Karol, and Kristina Podesva for their invaluable assistance.

At the Weatherspoon, thanks to preparators Susan Taaffe and Jack Stratton, and to Patti Gross, Shannon Byers, Cathy Rogers, and Maggie Gregory. Special thanks to Amy Howell, who organized the loans for this exhibition and its tour in record time.

Our greatest thanks go to Jim Hodges, who is an ideal collaborator. He has been generously available for studio visits, interviews, and site visits to our respective museums. His masterful touch and poetic sensibility bring life to this catalogue and exhibition. His art welcomes us and reminds us of the beauty of everyday experience, and as he says, "the wonder and greatness of all of life."

—IAN BERRY AND RON PLATT, CURATORS

This catalogue accompanies the exhibition

JIM HODGES

The Tang Teaching Museum and Art Gallery at Skidmore College
Saratoga Springs, New York
June 21–August 31, 2003

Austin Museum of Art
February 21–May 23, 2004

Weatherspoon Art Museum, The University of North Carolina at Greensboro
August 8–October 24, 2004

Museum of Contemporary Art, Cleveland
January 27–May 1, 2005

The Tang Teaching Museum and Art Gallery
Skidmore College
815 North Broadway
Saratoga Springs, New York 12866
T 518 580 8080
F 518 580 5069
www.skidmore.edu/tang

This exhibition and publication are made possible
in part with public funds from the New York State
Council on the Arts, a state agency, The Laurie Tisch
Sussman Foundation, The Overbrook Foundation,
and the Friends of the Tang. The catalogue is also
supported by Carla Chammas, Richard Desroche,
Glenn McMillan, and Carlos and Rosa de la Cruz.

©2003 The Frances Young Tang Teaching Museum
and Art Gallery at Skidmore College
ISBN 0-9725188-0-0
Library of Congress control number: 2003095378

Cover:
With, 1999
lightbulbs, ceramic sockets, wood and metal panels
31.5 x 63 x 5"
Private Collection, New York

Endpapers and bookmark by Jim Hodges

Page 1:
Visitors participating in *Wherever you like
(Possible Drawing)*, 1999
Miami Art Museum, Miami, Florida

Photographs:
Cover, pages 2, 4, 11, 12, 14, 22–23, 25, 26–27, 39,
44–45, 47, 49, 50, 52, 54–55, 59, 61, 62–63, 65,
74–75, 76–77, 78, 83, 85, 86–87, 88–89, 110:
Zindman/Fremont
Pages 1, 19: Juan Cabrera
Pages 6, 7, 8, 100, 107: Jim Hodges
Pages 16, 17, 108, 111: Liz Deschenes
Pages 29, 32–33, 42–43, 99, 106: Arthur Evans
Pages 34–35, 36–37, 113: Nancy Robinson Watson
Pages 40, 41, 105: Michael Tropea
Pages 90–91: Frank E. Graham

Designed by Bethany Johns
Printed in Germany by Cantz

this and this and that and this
and you and me and there and h
close and far, up and down, yes a
and never and always and sometin
now and this and that and alwa
never now and never again and perha
and soon and closer and then and
always something, never the right
and then yes and then no and then
not really, maybe, never, again
and again and again then and n
fast and slow so slow and long long
now and now and now and never a
and again and everything slow, e
tall things long things — tiny th
light dark dead and alive all things ev
now now now now now now a
all that is — ever was — ever wil
stay — stop and go and round an
everything into all — everything
everything, all every, all thin
this and this and this and that, that
and then and now right now —
just this and just now — just every
always more and more and more ev
right here now with you now always n